BREAKFAST

When thinking breakfast, the first thing that comes to mind – after coffee or tea, of course – is eggs. With an egg we can start the day right with a multitude of cooking ideas. We can scramble them, bake them, boil them, fry them or poach them. The old cry 'if there is an egg in the house there is a meal in the house' is just as true today as it was when first spoken over 100 years ago. However, we have not just stopped at eggs! We have provided a number of tasty dishes in this chapter, all easy to prepare and quickly cooked – so let's get started!

Baked eggs

100g/3½ oz spinach leaves, coarsely chopped
pinch of nutmeg
50g/1¾ oz salted ricotta, sliced
¼ cup thickened (whipping) cream
2 large eggs

1. Preheat the oven to 190°C/380°F.
2. Place two ramekins in a deep baking tray (sheet). Wash the spinach and cook with the nutmeg in a medium saucepan over low heat until wilted. Drain off excess water. Transfer the spinach to a medium bowl. Add the ricotta and cream and stir to combine. Spoon the spinach mixture into the ramekins and break an egg into the centre.
3. Fill the baking tray with boiling water to come halfway up the sides of the ramekins. Bake for 15 minutes, or until the eggs have set.

Serves 2 • Preparation 10 minutes • Cooking 15 minutes

French Toast with Strawberries

French toast with strawberries

3 large eggs
2 tablespoons milk
4 slices sourdough bread, about 2cm/¾ in thick
1½ cups strawberries, hulled and quartered
1 tablespoon icing (confectioner's) sugar

1. Preheat a large non-stick frying pan (skillet) on medium-high heat.
2. Beat the eggs and milk in a medium bowl until combined.
3. Dip the bread into the egg mixture, then cook for 3 minutes on each side until golden.
4. Place the French toast onto two serving plates. Top with strawberries and dust with icing (confectioner's) sugar.

Serves 2 • Preparation 5 minutes • Cooking 6 minutes

Porridge

¾ cup rolled oats
pinch of cinnamon
pinch of nutmeg
2 tablespoons brown sugar
⅓ cup milk

1. Place the oats and 1½ cups of water in a medium bowl. Cover and soak at room temperature overnight.
2. Transfer the oats and liquid to a medium saucepan. Add another ½ cup of water, the cinnamon and the nutmeg and bring to the boil. Reduce the heat and simmer, stirring, for 10 minutes or until the liquid has been absorbed. Divide the porridge between 2 serving bowls. Sprinkle with brown sugar and serve with cold milk.

Serves 2 • Preparation 12 hours • Cooking 15 minutes

Stuffed mushrooms

200g/7 oz baby spinach leaves
4 large field mushrooms, stalks trimmed
100g/3½ oz fetta cheese, crumbled
¼ cup sun-dried tomato pesto
freshly ground black pepper

1 Preheat the grill (broiler) to high.
2 Wash the spinach and cook in a medium saucepan over low heat until wilted.
3 Place the mushrooms on a baking tray (sheet), stem-side down, and grill for 3 minutes.
4 Turn the mushrooms over and top with wilted spinach. Sprinkle with fetta, pesto and freshly ground black pepper. Grill for a further 3 minutes, until mushrooms are cooked and cheese is golden.

Serves 2 • Preparation 6 minutes • Cooking 6 minutes

Bacon and avocado muffin

4 rashers bacon, halved and rind removed
2 English muffins, halved crosswise
2 tablespoons mayonnaise
½ teaspoon lemon pepper
1 ripe avocado, halved and stone removed

1 Preheat a medium non-stick frying pan (skillet) on medium-high heat. Cook the bacon for 2 minutes on each side or until crisp.
2 Toast the muffins in a toaster until golden brown. Spread mayonnaise on the muffin tops and sprinkle lemon pepper over.
3 Slice the avocado and lay on the base of the muffins. Top with bacon slices and cover with muffin tops.

Serves 2 • Preparation 5 minutes • Cooking 8 minutes

Stuffed Mushrooms

Smoked Salmon Bagel

Smoked salmon bagel

2 bagels, halved crosswise
4 tablespoons crème fraîche
2 slices smoked salmon
baby rocket (arugula) leaves
chopped chives

1 Preheat the grill (broiler) to high.
2 Grill the bagel on both sides until golden brown. Spread crème fraîche on both halves of the bagels. Lay smoked salmon slices on the bottom halves and top with rocket (arugula) and chives. Place the bagel lids on top and serve.

Serves 2 • Preparation 5 minutes • Cooking 5 minutes

Sausages and tomatoes

4 pork and fennel sausages
2 large ripe tomatoes, thickly sliced
4 tablespoons basil pesto
freshly ground black pepper
2 slices sourdough bread, about 2cm/¾ in thick

1 Preheat the grill (broiler) to medium.
2 Place the sausages on a grill tray (sheet) and cook, turning occasionally, for 15 minutes or until cooked.
3 Meanwhile, place the tomatoes on a small baking tray and spread with pesto and sprinkle with freshly ground black pepper. Cook under the grill for 5–10 minutes until they begin to soften. Toast the bread under the grill or in a toaster until golden brown.
4 Arrange the toast, sausages and tomatoes onto two serving plates.

Serves 2 • Preparation 10 minutes • Cooking 25 minutes

HAM AND CHEESE CROISSANT

2 croissants, halved crosswise
1 teaspoon French mustard
2 slices honey-cured ham
4 slices fontina or other mild cheese
3 tablespoons tomato chutney

1. Preheat the grill (broiler) to high.
2. Grill the croissants on both sides until golden. Spread French mustard on inside top halves of croissants.
3. Lay the ham slices on the bottom halves and top with cheese. Cook under the grill until the cheese has melted. Spread on the chutney, place the croissant lids on top and serve.

Serves 2 • Preparation 5 minutes • Cooking 8 minutes

Poached Eggs on Toast

Poached eggs on toast

4 large eggs
2 slices sourdough bread, about 2cm/¾ in thick
15g/½ oz butter
⅓ cup beetroot chutney
50g/1¾ oz rocket (arugula) leaves

1 Bring a medium saucepan of water to the simmer. Using a spoon, create a whirlpool and crack the eggs one at a time into the centre. Poach for about 3 minutes or until whites are slightly firm.

2 Cook the bread in a toaster until golden brown and spread with butter. Arrange the toast, eggs, rocket (arugula) and chutney onto two serving plates.

Serves 2 • Preparation 5 minutes • Cooking 6 minutes

Boiled eggs, bacon and black pudding

4 large eggs
45g/1½ oz butter, softened
200g/7 oz black pudding (blood sausage), sliced
1 rasher lean bacon
4 slices white bread

1 Cook the eggs in a medium saucepan of barely simmering water for 7 minutes. Drain well. Place the eggs in egg cups and cut off the tops.

2 Preheat a small non-stick frying pan (skillet) on medium heat. Melt one-third of the butter in the pan and cook the black pudding (blood sausage) for 2–3 minutes on each side until crisp and brown. Grill (broil) bacon and chop finely.

3 Cook the bread in a toaster until golden brown and spread with the remaining butter, top with the chopped bacon then serve with the eggs and black pudding.

Serves 2 • Preparation 6 minutes • Cooking 15 minutes

Creamed spinach and egg on toast

½ cup thickened (whipping) cream
pinch of nutmeg
200g/7 oz spinach, washed and chopped
4 large eggs
2 slices sourdough bread, about 2cm/¾ in thick

1. Place the cream, nutmeg and spinach in a large saucepan on medium heat. Cook for 5–10 minutes until the cream has thickened to a saucy consistency.
2. Meanwhile, bring a medium saucepan of water to the simmer. Using a spoon, create a whirlpool and crack the eggs one at a time into the centre. Poach for about 3 minutes, or until whites are slightly firm.
3. Cook the bread in a toaster until golden brown. Arrange the toast, creamed spinach and eggs onto two serving plates.

Serves 2 • Preparation 10 minutes • Cooking 15 minutes

Basil and Fetta Omelette

4 large eggs, separated
½ cup fresh basil leaves, torn
90g/3 oz fetta cheese, crumbled
½ red onion, sliced
2 tablespoons olive oil

1. Preheat the grill (broiler) to medium-high.
2. Beat the egg yolks in a medium bowl. In a separate bowl, whisk the whites until soft peaks form. Gently fold the whites through the yolks until combined.
3. Preheat the oil in a small non-stick frying pan (skillet) on medium heat. Spoon half the egg mixture into the pan and cook for 1 minute. Place the pan under the hot grill and cook the top of the omelette for a further 1–2 minutes or until set and golden. Set aside and keep warm. Repeat the process for the remaining egg mixture. Serve topped with basil, fetta and red onion.

Serves 2 • Preparation 5 minutes • Cooking 5 minutes

Potato cakes

350g/12 oz potatoes, peeled and quartered
1 tablespoon cream
45g/1½ oz butter
¾ cup plain (all-purpose) flour
4 tablespoons strawberry jam (jelly)

1 Place the potatoes in a medium saucepan. Cover with cold water and bring to the boil. Cook for 8–10 minutes or until tender. Drain well and return to the saucepan. Add the cream and one-third of the butter and mash. Leave to cool slightly.

2 Turn the mash out onto a clean, floured work surface. Gradually add the flour, kneading until a smooth dough is formed. Roll out to 1cm/⅓ in thickness and cut into triangles.

3 Preheat a large frying pan (skillet) on medium heat. Melt the remaining butter in the pan and cook the potato cakes for 3 minutes on each side or until browned. Serve hot with strawberry jam (jelly).

Serves 2 • Preparation 10 minutes • Cooking 16 minutes

Waffles with banana

15g/½ oz butter
2 bananas, peeled and halved lengthwise
4 waffles
⅓ cup vanilla yoghurt
2 tablespoons maple syrup

1 Melt the butter in a non-stick frying pan (skillet).

2 Add the bananas and cook on medium-low heat for 2 minutes on each side or until golden brown.

3 Meanwhile, cook the waffles in a toaster until warmed and golden brown.

4 Arrange waffles on two serving plates. Place the cooked bananas on top and dollop with yoghurt. Drizzle with maple syrup and serve.

Serves 2 • Preparation 5 minutes • Cooking 5 minutes

Potato Cakes

Blueberries and Yoghurt

BLUEBERRIES AND YOGHURT

100g/3½ oz pecans
2 cups vanilla yoghurt
1 teaspoon honey
1 teaspoon ground cinnamon
3 cups blueberries

1. Preheat the oven to 180°C/360°F.
2. Spread the pecans on a baking tray (sheet) and toast in the oven for 10 minutes or until lightly toasted. Coarsely chop.
3. Combine the yoghurt, honey and cinnamon in a small bowl. Layer the yoghurt, blueberries and pecans in two glass serving bowls or cups.

Serves 2 • Preparation 5 minutes • Cooking 10 minutes

BIRCHER MUESLI

1 cup rolled oats
1 cup apple juice
1 apple, grated
¼ teaspoon cinnamon
½ cup natural yoghurt

1. Place the oats and apple juice in a bowl. Cover with plastic wrap and soak for 2 hours or overnight in the refrigerator.
2. Stir through the grated apple, cinnamon and yoghurt. Divide amongst two serving bowls.

Serves 2 • Preparation 2 hours 5 minutes

FRUIT SALAD

¼ seedless watermelon
¼ rockmelon (cantaloupe)
4 kiwifruit, peeled
250g/9 oz strawberries, hulled and halved
whipped (double) cream to serve, optional

1 Remove the skins from the melon pieces. Scrape the seeds out of the rockmelon (cantaloupe). Slice the melons into lengths and place in a medium bowl. Slice each kiwifruit into eight lengthwise. Add the kiwifruit and strawberries to the melons and stir to combine.

2 Divide the fruit salad amongst four serving bowls and serve with whipped (double) cream if desired.

Serves 4 • Preparation 5 minutes

BANANA AND HONEY SMOOTHIE

2 large ripe bananas, peeled
1 cup milk
¾ cup plain yoghurt
1 tablespoon honey
4 tablespoons LSA (ground linseed, sunflower seed and almond meal mix)

1 Cut the bananas into pieces and place in a food processor or blender. Add the milk, yoghurt, honey and LSA. Blend until smooth and thick.

2 Pour the smoothie into two large glasses to serve.

Serves 2 • Preparation 5 minutes

Fruit Salad

DIPS & SAUCES

DIPS & SAUCES

At your next dinner party, why not make up a tasty dip to start the occasion, or maybe just a few drinks with a dip to tease the palate? And how about using one of these great sauce recipes? There's a mint sauce to go with your lamb, mayonnaise to go with chicken, cocktail sauce to suit fresh seafood, or a salsa for that great barbecued steak. The ideas here are simple, easy to prepare and most of all are very tasty indeed.

Eggplant Dip

Eggplant dip

2 medium eggplants (aubergines)
4 tablespoons extra virgin olive oil
1 clove garlic, finely chopped
2 tablespoons lemon juice
1 French baguette, cut into 1cm/⅓ in slices

1 Preheat the grill (broiler) to high.

2 Prick the eggplants (aubergines) with a knife to prevent them from bursting. Place under the grill and cook for 5 minutes, turning occasionally, until soft. Peel the eggplant and place the flesh in a colander. Mash to a purée using a fork or the back of a spoon, allowing the juices to drain out.

3 Transfer the eggplant purée to a medium bowl. Add the olive oil, garlic and lemon juice, stirring to combine. Serve in a small bowl accompanied with chunks of bread.

Serves 4 • Preparation 5 minutes • Cooking 5 minutes

Spiced yoghurt dip

½ teaspoon cumin seeds
¼ teaspoon ground turmeric
pinch of allspice
300g/10½ oz natural yoghurt
1 tablespoon lemon juice

1 Cook the spices in a small frying pan (skillet) over medium heat until fragrant. Remove from the heat and leave to cool.

2 Place the yoghurt in a small bowl. Add the spices and lemon juice and stir to combine. Transfer to a small serving dish.

Serves 4 • Preparation 5 minutes • Cooking 5 minutes

Beetroot and Sour Cream Dip

3 medium beetroots, trimmed
1 clove garlic, crushed
¾ cup sour cream
1 tablespoon lemon juice
¼ small bunch chives, cut into 3cm/1¼ in batons

1 Cook the beetroots in a medium saucepan of boiling water for 35 minutes or until tender. Drain and leave to cool.

2 Peel the beetroots, wearing food handling gloves to prevent staining your hands. Coarsely chop and place in a food processor with the garlic. Add the sour cream and lemon juice and purée until smooth. Transfer to a small serving dish and garnish with chives.

Serves 4 • Preparation 10 minutes • Cooking 35 minutes

Guacamole

2 ripe avocados
3 tablespoons lemon juice
1 clove garlic, crushed
¼ teaspoon chopped chilli
1 small red onion, finely diced

1 Cut the avocados lengthwise and discard the stones. Scoop out the flesh with a large spoon and place in a medium bowl. Add the lemon juice garlic and chilli. Mash with the back of a fork until fairly smooth. Stir through the onion and transfer to a small serving dish. Cover with plastic wrap and chill until ready to serve.

Serves 4 • Preparation 10 minutes • Cooking 10 minutes

Beetroot and Sour Cream Dip

White Bean Dip

WHITE BEAN DIP

400g/14 oz canned cannellini (white kidney) beans, drained
2 tablespoons lemon juice
2 tablespoons extra virgin olive oil
½ teaspoon ground cumin
½ teaspoon ground black pepper

1 Place the cannellini (white kidney) beans, lemon juice, olive oil, cumin and black pepper in a food processor. Process until smooth, adding a little water if it's too thick. Transfer to a small serving dish.

Serves 4 • Preparation 10 minutes

TARAMASALATA

200g/7 oz fresh smoked cod roe
½ teaspoon ground black pepper
1 slice white bread, crust removed
1 tablespoon lemon juice
1 cup light olive oil

1 Place the roe in a small bowl, cover with cold water and soak for 2 hours. Drain, peel off the skin and place the roe in a food processor with the black pepper.

2 Moisten the bread with cold water and squeeze out any excess. Add the bread and lemon juice to the roe and pulse until puréed. With processor on medium-high speed, gradually pour in the oil. Go slowly otherwise it will curdle. Scrape down the sides and process until combined and thick. Transfer to a small serving dish.

Serves 4 • Preparation 2 hours 10 minutes

Skordalia

500g/1 lb potatoes
8 cloves garlic, crushed
½ cup extra virgin olive oil
2 tablespoons lemon juice
½ teaspoon lemon pepper

1 Peel and cut the potatoes into cubes. Place in a medium saucepan, cover with water and bring to the boil. Cook for 10–15 minutes until tender. Drain and leave to cool a little.

2 Place the potato, garlic, olive oil, lemon juice and pepper in a food processor. Blend until smooth and creamy. Add a little of the cooking water if it's too thick.

Serves 4 • Preparation 10 minutes • Cooking 15 minutes

Smoked salmon dip

80g/2¾ oz smoked salmon
1 teaspoon lemon juice
1 tablespoon capers
200g/7 oz cream cheese, softened
¼ cup sour cream

1 Place the smoked salmon, lemon juice and capers in a food processor and pulse until finely chopped. Add the cream cheese and sour cream and process until smooth.

Serves 4 • Preparation 5 minutes

Skordalia

Blue Cheese and Walnut Dip

Blue cheese and walnut dip

150g/5 oz soft blue cheese
200g/7 oz crème fraîche
75g/2½ oz walnuts, lightly toasted and coarsely chopped
¼ cup fresh basil leaves, finely chopped
crisp crunchy bread to dip

1 Place the blue cheese and half the crème fraîche in a small bowl. Stir until combined. Add the remaining crème fraîche, walnuts and basil and mix well. Garnish with a few extra walnuts. Serve with crunchy bread to dip.

Serves 4 • Preparation 5 minutes

Spicy sambal dip

4 red capsicums (peppers)
1 clove garlic, crushed
¼ cup extra virgin olive oil
1 tablespoon lemon juice
2 teaspoons sambal oelek

1 Preheat the grill (broiler) to high. Grill the capsicums (peppers) until the skins have blackened all over. Place in a bowl and cover with plastic wrap for 10 minutes. Remove the skins and seeds and discard, then coarsely chop the flesh.

2 Place the capsicum, garlic, olive oil, lemon juice and sambal oelek in a food processor. Blend until smooth, then transfer to a small serving dish.

Serves 4 • Preparation 20 minutes • Cooking 10 minutes

Mexican salsa

1 green capsicum (pepper), halved lengthwise
and deseeded
2 large red chillies, halved lengthwise
and deseeded
1 clove garlic, crushed
2 large ripe tomatoes, diced
3 tablespoons extra virgin olive oil

1 Chop the capsicum (pepper) and finely chop the chilli. Combine the capsicum, chilli, garlic, tomato and olive oil in a medium bowl. Stir to combine. Transfer to a small serving bowl.

Serves 4 • Preparation 5 minutes

Tapenade

150g/5 oz pitted black (ripe) olives
100g/3½ oz balsamic Kalamata olives
1 clove garlic, crushed
2 tablespoons capers
1 tablespoon lemon juice

1 Place the olives, garlic, capers and lemon juice in a food processor. Blend until smooth. Transfer to a small serving bowl.

Serves 4 • Preparation 5 minutes

Mexican Salsa

Artichoke Dip

Artichoke dip

1 large red onion
400g/14 oz marinated artichokes, drained and liquid reserved
4 capers
200g/7 oz cream cheese
4 sprigs fresh oregano, leaves removed and finely chopped

1 Preheat the oven to 190°C/380°F.
2 Place the onion on a small baking tray (sheet) and roast for 35–40 minutes until softened. Leave to cool a little, then peel and coarsely chop.
3 Place the onion, artichokes, capers and cream cheese in a food processor. Blend until smooth, adding a little of the reserved liquid if it's too thick. Stir through the oregano and transfer to a small serving dish.

Serves 4 • Preparation 10 minutes • Cooking 40 minutes

Mint and citrus raita

300g/10½ oz natural yoghurt
¼ cup fresh coriander (cilantro) leaves, finely chopped
¼ cup fresh mint leaves, finely chopped
½ tablespoon lime juice
½ tablespoon lemon juice

1 Place the yoghurt in a small bowl, then add the coriander (cilantro) and mint. Add the lime and lemon juice and stir to combine. Transfer to a small serving dish.

Serves 4 • Preparation 5 minutes

Mint sauce

⅓ cup fresh mint leaves
⅛ teaspoon ground rock salt
1 tablespoon sugar
¼ cup malt vinegar
¼ cup cider vinegar

1 Finely chop the mint and place in a medium bowl.

2 Place ¼ cup water, the salt and sugar in a small saucepan over medium heat and bring to the boil. Remove from the heat and add the vinegars. Pour liquid over the mint and leave to cool. Transfer to a serving jug.

Serves 4 • Preparation 5 minutes • Cooking 5 minutes

Gremolata

¼ cup flat-leaf parsley, finely chopped
¼ cup fresh mint leaves, finely chopped
finely chopped zest of 4 large lemons
freshly ground black pepper
2 cloves garlic, crushed

1 Place the parsley and mint leaves in a medium bowl. Add the lemon zest, pepper and garlic and stir to combine. Transfer to a small serving dish.

Serves 4 • Preparation 5 minutes

Mint Sauce

Sweet and Spicy Dip

Sweet and spicy dip

2 sweet potatoes (yams), peeled and diced
1 large red chilli, finely chopped with seeds
2cm/¾ in piece ginger (gingerroot), thinly sliced
⅓ teaspoon ground nutmeg
2 teaspoons sesame oil

1. Place the sweet potato (yam), chilli and ginger (gingerroot) in a medium saucepan. Cover with cold water and bring to the boil over medium heat. Decrease the heat, cover and gently simmer for 10 minutes or until softened. Drain in a colander and leave to cool.
2. Put the sweet potato mixture into a food processor with the nutmeg. Add the sesame oil and process until smooth. Serve in a small bowl.

Serves 4 • Preparation 10 minutes • Cooking 15 minutes

Cocktail sauce

1 cup mayonnaise
½ tablespoon thickened (whipping) cream
¼ cup tomato sauce (ketchup)
1 tablespoon Worcestershire sauce
1 tablespoon lemon juice

1. Place all the ingredients in a small bowl and stir to combine. Transfer to a small serving dish.

Serves 4 • Preparation 5 minutes • Cooking 10 minutes

Lentil dip

250g/9 oz yellow or red lentils
1½ teaspoons cumin seeds
1 clove garlic, minced
½ tablespoon lemon juice
3 tablespoons extra virgin olive oil

1 Place the lentils in a medium saucepan and cover with double their volume of water. Bring to the boil and cook for 15 minutes. Add more water if necessary and continue cooking until they form a soft purée. Leave to cool.

2 Cook the cumin seeds in a small frying pan (skillet) over medium heat until fragrant. Add 1 teaspoon of the cumin seeds, the garlic, lemon juice and olive oil to the lentil purée. Stir to combine. Transfer to a small serving bowl and garnish with the remaining cumin seeds.

Serves 4 • Preparation 10 minutes • Cooking 25 minutes

Garlic aïoli

1 large bulb garlic
1 cup mayonnaise
1 tablespoon lemon juice
¼ teaspoon lemon pepper
¼ cup parsley, finely chopped

1 Preheat the oven to 190°C/380°F.

2 Place the garlic bulb on a small roasting tray and roast for 30 minutes or until soft. Leave to cool. Squeeze the garlic out of its skin into a small bowl, then mash with the back of a fork.

3 Add the mayonnaise, lemon juice, lemon pepper and parsley and stir to combine.

Serves 4 • Preparation 5 minutes • Cooking 30 minutes

Lentil Dip

Tartare Sauce

Tartare sauce

1 cup mayonnaise
1 large gherkin (pickled cucumber/dill pickle), finely chopped
1 tablespoon capers, finely chopped
1 tablespoon lemon juice
¼ teaspoon ground white pepper

1 Place the mayonnaise in a small bowl, then add the gherkin (pickled cucumber/dill pickle) and capers. Pour in the lemon juice and white pepper and stir to combine. Transfer to a small serving dish.

Serves 4 • Preparation 5 minutes

Mayonnaise

3 large egg yolks, at room temperature
1 teaspoon Dijon mustard
¼ teaspoon ground white pepper
2 tablespoons lemon juice
¾ cup sunflower or canola oil

1 Place the egg yolks, mustard, pepper and lemon juice in a food processor and pulse to combine. With the motor running, add the oil in a thin stream until incorporated. Add a little hot water if mayonnaise is too thick. Transfer to a serving dish or storage jar and refrigerate.

Mayonnaise will keep for about 1 week in the refrigerator.

Serves 4 • Preparation 10 minutes

SEAFOOD, POULTRY & MEAT

Seafood, Poultry & Meat

With so many different varieties of seafood, poultry and meat available, you can easily get overwhelmed when deciding what to choose to make an interesting, tasty meal. In this chapter, we have produced very simple dishes that can be prepared with the minimum of fuss and ingredients, yet they are as tasty as those that require a multitude of ingredients. This will not only save you time but will also make it easier to select something that will suit your budget.

BAKED FISH IN PASTRY

12 sheets filo pastry
100g/3½ oz butter, melted
4 John Dory fillets, about 200g/7 oz each
6 tablespoons coriander (cilantro) pesto
½ lemon, sliced thinly

1 Preheat the oven to 200°C/400°F.

2 Cover the sheets of filo with a clean, slightly damp tea towel to prevent them from drying out while you are working.

3 Place a sheet of filo on a dry, flat work surface and brush with melted butter. Repeat the process until you have three layered sheets. Place a piece of fish 5cm/2 in in from the edge, folding the tail under if necessary to create an even thickness. Spread 1½ tablespoons of coriander (cilantro) pesto and half lemon slices over the fish. Fold the filo over the fish, tucking the edges underneath to seal. Brush with butter and repeat the process with the remaining pastry, fish, lemon and pesto.

4 Line a large baking tray (sheet) with baking paper. Place the filo parcels on the tray and bake for 20 minutes or until pastry is golden brown and the fish is cooked through.

Serves 4 • Preparation 20 minutes • Cooking 20 minutes

MARINATED OCTOPUS SALAD

1¼ kg/2¾ lb baby octopus
⅓ cup olive oil
1 clove garlic, crushed
⅓ cup lemon juice
150g/5 oz curly endive leaves (chicory)

1 Remove and discard the heads and beaks from the octopus, then cut each one in half.

2 Combine the olive oil, garlic and lemon juice in a large bowl. Add the octopus and toss to coat. Cover with plastic wrap and refrigerate for 2 hours or until required. Drain the octopus and reserve the marinade.

3 Preheat the barbeque plate to high. Cook the octopus for 2–3 minutes, stirring frequently and basting with the reserved marinade.

4 Place the endive (chicory) in a large bowl. Add the octopus and toss to combine.

Serves 4 • Preparation 2 hours 20 minutes • Cooking 5 minutes

Scallops with Capers and Lemon

32 scallops, in half shells
3 tablespoons capers, finely chopped
juice and finely grated zest of 2 lemons
60g/2 oz butter, cubed
freshly ground black pepper

1. Preheat the grill (broiler) to high.
2. Loosen the scallops from their shells by sliding a small knife between the shell and the scallop. Arrange the scallops on baking trays (sheets).
3. Combine the capers, lemon zest and juice in a small bowl. Spoon the caper mixture over the scallops and top each with a small cube of butter.
4. Grill the scallops for 4 minutes, or until cooked through. Arrange on four serving plates and sprinkle with black pepper.

Serves 4 • Preparation 10 minutes • Cooking 4 minutes

Barramundi with Mango

2 mangoes, peeled
2 limes
1 lemon
¾ cup fresh coriander (cilantro) leaves
4 barramundi (Asian seabass) fillets, about 200g/7 oz each

1 Dice the mango and place in a medium bowl. Finely chop the zest from 1 lime, then squeeze the juice from it and the lemon. Combine coriander (cilantro) leaves, lime zest and juice, and lemon juice, then toss through the mango. Cut the remaining lime into quarters.

2 Preheat a large non-stick frying pan (skillet) on medium-high heat. Cook the fish for 2 minutes on each side or until flesh flakes easily. Serve immediately with mango and the lime wedges.

Serves 4 • Preparation 10 minutes • Cooking 4 minutes

Baked Thyme-Stuffed Whole Trout

1kg/2 lb baby (new) potatoes
¼ cup olive oil
4 small whole trout, scaled and cleaned
juice of 1 lemon
2 bunches thyme, washed and ends trimmed

1 Preheat the oven to 190°C/380°F.

2 Place the potatoes in a medium saucepan. Cover with cold water and bring to the boil. Cook for 5 minutes, then drain and place on a large baking tray (sheet). Pour over 4 tablespoons of the olive oil and toss to coat. Roast for 20–25 minutes until golden brown.

3 Meanwhile, tear off four pieces of aluminium foil large enough to wrap each trout. Score the trout 3 times on each side. Drizzle over the remaining oil and place the fish onto the foil. Pour lemon juice over it. Sprinkle a few thyme leaves over the fish and stuff the remaining thyme inside the cavity. Enclose the trout in the foil and place onto baking trays. Bake for 15–20 minutes until flesh flakes easily. Serve with the potatoes.

Serves 4 • Preparation 20 minutes • Cooking 50 minutes

Steamed fish with ginger and lime

1½ cups basmati rice
5cm/2 in piece ginger (gingerroot), peeled and sliced
12 kaffir lime leaves, finely sliced
¼ teaspoon ground coriander
4 firm white fish fillets, about 200g/7 oz each

1. Combine the rice with 2¼ cups water in a saucepan. Bring to the boil, reduce heat to low, cover and cook for 15 minutes. Remove pan from heat, allow to stand covered for 10 minutes.
2. Meanwhile, line a large steamer with parchment. Make holes in the paper so that the steam can penetrate. Fill the base of the steamer with 4cm/1½ in of water, place over high heat, bring to the boil, then reduce to a simmer.
3. Sprinkle half the ginger (gingerroot), half the lime leaves and the coriander on the prepared paper and place the fish on top. Top with the remaining ginger and lime, cover and cook for 6–10 minutes until the flesh flakes easily. Serve the fish immediately with rice.

Serves 4 • Preparation 25 minutes • Cooking 25 minutes

TERIYAKI FISH

4 marlin steaks, about 150g/5 oz each
1 cup teriyaki sauce
1 tablespoon freshly grated ginger (gingerroot)
1½ cups basmati rice
4 spring (green) onions, trimmed

1 Place the fish in a medium bowl and coat in teriyaki sauce and ginger (gingerroot). Cover and refrigerate for 1 hour.

2 Combine the rice with 2¼ cups water in a saucepan. Bring to the boil, reduce heat to low, cover and cook for 15 minutes. Remove pan from heat, allow to stand covered for 10 minutes.

3 Cut the spring (green) onions into 6cm/2½ in batons. Thinly slice the batons lengthwise into strips.

4 Preheat a large non-stick frying pan (skillet) over medium-high heat. Take the fish out of the marinade, reserving the marinade, and cook for 2 minutes on each side or until browned. Add the reserved marinade and gently simmer, basting until the fish is covered in a glossy glaze.

5 Divide the rice and fish evenly amongst four serving plates or bowls and top with spring onions.

Serves 4 • Preparation 1 hour 25 minutes • Cooking 25 minutes

FISH WITH THAI RED CURRY SAUCE

1½ tablespoons red curry paste
1 cup coconut milk
½ teaspoon ground coriander
8 baby bok choy, halved lengthwise
4 firm white fish fillets, about 200g/7 oz each

1 Preheat a large non-stick frying pan (skillet) over medium heat. Add the curry paste and cook until aromatic. Pour in the coconut milk and coriander, reduce the heat and gently simmer for 2 minutes until thickened slightly.

2 Meanwhile, fill the base of a steamer with 4cm/1½ in of water and place over high heat, bring to the boil and then reduce to a simmer. Place the bok choy on the steamer tray, cover and cook for 3 minutes or until tender. Add the fillets to the curry sauce and cook, basting with sauce for 3–4 minutes until cooked through.

3 Carefully lift the fish out of the sauce and place on serving plates with the bok choy. Pour over the sauce and serve.

Serves 4 · Preparation 15 minutes · Cooking 10 minutes

Baked tuna steaks with fennel and tomato

800g/28 oz canned chopped Roma tomatoes
zest of 1 lemon
1 head fennel, thinly sliced
2 cloves garlic, finely chopped
4 tuna steaks, about 180g/6½ oz each

1. Preheat the oven to 200°C/400°F.
2. Place the tomatoes, lemon zest, fennel and garlic in a medium bowl and stir to combine.
3. Spoon half the fennel and tomato mixture into a large ovenproof baking dish. Place the fish on top and spoon over the remaining mixture. Cover and bake for 25 minutes or until cooked through.

Serves 4 • Preparation 10 minutes • Cooking 25 minutes

TAPENADE-CRUSTED FISH

4 skinless firm white fish fillets, about 200g/7 oz each
¼ tablespoon freshly ground black pepper
8 medium vine-ripened tomatoes
¾ cup Japanese panko crumbs
8 tablespoons tapenade (see page 42)

1. Preheat the oven to 200°C/400°F.
2. Line a baking tray (sheet) with baking paper and place the fillets on top, sprinkle with pepper.
3. Place the tomatoes on a separate baking tray and bake for 10–15 minutes, until they begin to soften.
4. Meanwhile, combine the panko crumbs and tapenade in a small bowl. Press a layer of crumb mixture on top of each fillet. Bake for 8–10 minutes until crumbs are golden and fish is cooked through. Serve with roasted tomatoes.

Serves 4 • Preparation 15 minutes • Cooking 25 minutes

Sardines with Tomato Salsa

6 medium tomatoes, diced
1 cup pitted black (ripe) olives, chopped
juice of 1 lemon
4 tablespoons olive oil
12 sardines, scaled and cleaned

1. Place the tomatoes, olives, lemon juice and half the oil in a medium bowl. Toss to combine.
2. Preheat a large non-stick frying pan (skillet) over medium-high heat. Brush the sardines with the remaining oil. Cook the sardines for 2 minutes on each side or until cooked through.
3. Divide the sardines and salsa amongst four serving plates.

Serves 4 • Preparation 5 minutes • Cooking 4 minutes

Baked Salmon with Pesto, Potatoes and Beans

1kg/2 lb baby (new) potatoes, thickly sliced
4 salmon cutlets, skin on, about 180g/6½ oz each
350g/12 oz green beans, trimmed and halved
½ cup pesto
¼ cup fresh basil, chopped

1. Preheat the oven to 200°C/400°F.
2. Place the potatoes in a medium saucepan. Cover with cold water and bring to the boil. Cook for 5–8 minutes or until tender.
3. Meanwhile, place the salmon on a baking tray (sheet). Bake for 8–10 minutes or until just cooked.
4. Bring a medium saucepan of water to the boil. Blanch the beans for 2 minutes.
5. Drain the potatoes and beans, combine in a large bowl and toss through the pesto and basil. Divide the vegetables and fish evenly amongst four serving plates.

Serves 4 • Preparation 15 minutes • Cooking 20 minutes

Oysters Kilpatrick

2 dozen oysters in half shells
1 bag rock salt
4 tablespoons Worcestershire sauce
1 teaspoon hot sauce
6 rashers rindless bacon, finely chopped

1. Preheat the grill (broiler) to high.
2. Cover two oven trays (sheets) with rock salt. Place the oysters in their shells in the salt to stabilise them.
3. Combine the Worcestershire and hot sauce in a small bowl. Spoon the sauce over the oysters and top with bacon.
4. Cook the oysters under the grill for 3 minutes or until the bacon has begun to crisp.
5. Spread rock salt onto four serving plates and arrange the oysters in their shells on top. Serve immediately.

Serves 4 • Preparation 10 minutes • Cooking 6 minutes

CHILLI SEAFOOD NOODLES

24 raw tiger prawns (shrimp)
3 tablespoons sambal oelek
400g/14 oz vermicelli rice noodles
2 tablespoons vegetable oil
2 red capsicums (peppers), deseeded and thinly sliced

1. Remove the heads and shells from the prawns (shrimp), leaving the tails intact. Place the prawns in a medium bowl, add the sambal oelek and toss to coat. Cover and refrigerate for 1–2 hours.
2. Place the noodles in a medium bowl, cover with boiling water and soak for 5–10 minutes until softened. Drain and set aside.
3. Heat the oil in a large non-stick frying pan (skillet) over high heat. Cook the prawns for 1½ minutes on each side or until they turn pink and begin to firm up. Add the capsicum (pepper) and the noodles and toss to combine. Serve immediately.

Serves 4 • Preparation 2 hours 25 minutes • Cooking 15 minutes

Chicken, Fennel and Orange Salad

1 tablespoon vegetable oil
4 chicken breast fillets
3 oranges
1 fennel bulb, core removed and thinly sliced
150g/5 oz watercress

1. Heat the oil in a large non-stick frying pan (skillet) on medium-high heat.
2. Cook the chicken breasts for 5–7 minutes on each side until cooked through. Remove from the heat and leave to rest for 5 minutes.
3. Meanwhile, peel and segment the oranges over a bowl, collecting the juice that drips as you work.
4. Slice the chicken and place in a large bowl. Add the orange segments, fennel and watercress. Pour in enough of the reserved orange juice to moisten as a dressing. Toss to combine and serve.

Serves 4 • Preparation 20 minutes • Cooking 20 minutes

ROAST LEMON CHICKEN WITH COUSCOUS

1 whole chicken, about 2kg/4.4 lb
3 lemons
1¾ cups chicken stock (broth)
2 sprigs thyme
1½ cups couscous

1. Preheat the oven 190°C/380°F.
2. Remove any excess fat from the chicken cavity. Tie the chicken legs together using unwaxed kitchen string and place in a large roasting pan.
3. Juice two of the lemons into a small bowl and add ¼ cup of the chicken stock (broth). Pour over the chicken. Cut the remaining lemon in half and place one half in the chicken cavity with the thyme. Slice the remaining half and arrange over the chicken. Roast, basting occasionally, for 1½ hours or until juices run clear from the thigh when pricked with a skewer.
4. Meanwhile, pour the chicken stock into a small saucepan and bring to the boil. Add the couscous, remove from the heat and cover with plastic wrap. Leave to stand for 5 minutes or until liquid is completely absorbed. Stir gently with a fork to separate the grains.
5. Serve the roast chicken with couscous.

Serves 4 · Preparation 20 minutes · Cooking 1 hour 35 minutes

Garlic chicken

90g/3 oz butter, softened
6 cloves garlic, crushed
1 tablespoon oregano leaves
½ cup fresh parsley leaves, finely chopped
4 chicken breasts on the bone, skin on

1. Preheat the oven to 180°C/360°F.
2. Place the butter, garlic, oregano and parsley in a small bowl and stir to combine.
3. Put the garlic butter under the chicken skin. Place the chicken breasts skin-side up and bake for 20–25 minutes until cooked through.

Serves 4 • Preparation 10 minutes • Cooking 25 minutes

Sweet Orange Chicken

4 skinless chicken breast fillets
6 tablespoons orange marmalade
zest of 1 lemon
150g/5 oz baby rocket (arugula) leaves
80g/2¾ oz fetta cheese, cubed

1. Preheat the oven to 180°C/360°F.
2. Place the chicken breasts on a large baking tray (sheet) lined with baking paper. Coat each breast with the orange marmalade and lemon zest. Cover with foil and bake for 10 minutes. Remove the foil and bake for a further 10–15 minutes or until cooked through.
3. Serve the chicken with the rocket (arugula) and fetta.

Serves 4 • Preparation 10 minutes • Cooking 25 minutes

Chicken yakitori

1kg/2 lb chicken thigh fillets, cut into 3cm/1¼ in pieces
¾ cup teriyaki sauce
1½ cups basmati rice
3 tablespoons sesame seeds, toasted
1 teaspoon sesame oil

1. Place the chicken pieces in a medium bowl. Add the teriyaki sauce and toss to coat. Cover and refrigerate for 1–2 hours or until required.
2. Carefully thread the chicken onto skewers.
3. Preheat a grill (broiler) plate on medium-high heat.
4. Combine the rice with 2¼ cups water in a saucepan. Bring to the boil, reduce heat to low, cover and cook for 15 minutes. Remove pan from heat, allow to stand covered for 10 minutes. Stir through the toasted sesame seeds.
5. Meanwhile, brush the yakitori with sesame oil and cook for 5 minutes on each side or until cooked through. Serve with the rice.

Serves 4 • Preparation 2 hours 25 minutes • Cooking 20 minutes

CHINESE BARBECUE DUCK WITH BOK CHOY AND NOODLES

400g/14 oz udon noodles
6 heads bok choy, quartered lengthwise
1 teaspoon sesame oil
1 Chinese barbecue duck, meat sliced off the bone
2 tablespoons tamari (wheat-free soy sauce)

1 Cook the noodles in a large pot of boiling water according to packet instructions. Drain and set aside.

2 Fill the base of a steamer with 4cm/1½ in of water, place over high heat, bring to the boil and then reduce to a simmer. Place the bok choy on the steamer tray, cover and cook for 3 minutes or until tender.

3 Heat the oil in a large non-stick frying pan (skillet) or wok on medium-high heat. Add the duck and toss to warm through. Add the noodles, bok choy and tamari (wheat-free soy sauce) and toss to combine. Divide evenly amongst four serving bowls.

Serves 4 • Preparation 20 minutes • Cooking 20 minutes

DUCK WITH PLUM SAUCE

4 duck breasts
1 teaspoon kecap (ketjap) manis
½ cup Asian plum sauce
1½ cups basmati rice
4 pak choy, trimmed and leaves separated

1. Use a sharp knife to score the skin of the duck breasts at 1cm/⅓ in intervals. Place the duck in a medium bowl with kecap (ketjap) manis and plum sauce and coat duck. Cover with plastic wrap and refrigerate for 1–2 hours or until required.
2. Combine the rice with 2¼ cups water in a saucepan. Bring to the boil, reduce heat to low, cover and cook for 15 minutes. Remove pan from heat, allow to stand covered for 10 minutes.
3. Preheat the oven to 180°C/360°F. Preheat a large non-stick frying pan (skillet) over medium-high heat. Cook the duck, skin-side down, for 3 minutes or until golden brown. Turn over and cook for a further minute. Transfer to an ovenproof dish and bake for 8 minutes for medium, or until cooked to your liking. Cover with foil and rest for 5 minutes.
4. Meanwhile, place a medium saucepan of water on high heat and bring to the boil. Blanch the pak choy for 1 minute, then drain. Serve the duck with rice and pak choy.

Serves 4 • Preparation 2 hours 20 minutes • Cooking 30 minutes

Sweet Chilli Chicken and Rice Noodle Salad

1 tablespoon vegetable oil
2 chicken breast fillets
400g/14 oz vermicelli rice noodles
250g/9 oz snowpeas (mange tout)
½ cup sweet chilli sauce

1. Heat the oil in a large non-stick frying pan (skillet) on medium-high heat.
2. Cook the chicken breasts for 5–7 minutes on each side until cooked through. Remove from the heat and leave to rest for 5 minutes.
3. Meanwhile, place the noodles in a medium bowl, cover with boiling water and soak until softened. Drain and set aside.
4. Blanch the snowpeas (mange tout) in boiling water for 30 seconds. Plunge into iced water to stop the cooking process. Slice thinly lengthwise.
5. Shred the chicken and place in a large bowl. Add the noodles, snowpeas and sweet chilli sauce. Toss to combine and serve.

Serves 4 • Preparation 20 minutes • Cooking 22 minutes

Honey Mustard Chicken with Roast Potatoes

4 chicken leg quarters
¾ cup honey mustard marinade
500g/1 lb baby (new) potatoes
3 tablespoons olive oil
1 tablespoon lemon juice

1. Place the chicken in a medium bowl and coat with marinade. Cover with plastic wrap and refrigerate for 2 hours or until required.
2. Preheat the oven to 200°C/400°F.
3. Place the potatoes in a large saucepan and cover with water. Bring to the boil and cook for 5 minutes. Drain and place in a roasting dish. Pour in the olive oil and lemon juice and toss to coat. Roast for 30 minutes or until golden brown.
4. Meanwhile, preheat a large non-stick frying pan (skillet) on medium-high heat. Cook the chicken legs for 2 minutes on each side or until browned. Transfer to an ovenproof dish and bake for 20 minutes or until cooked through. Serve the chicken with the roast potatoes.

Serves 4 • Preparation 2 hours 20 minutes • Cooking 30 minutes

Chicken and Hokkien Noodles

400g/14 oz hokkien noodles
3 chicken thigh fillets, sliced
1 bunch gai lan (Chinese broccoli), cut into short lengths
1 clove garlic, crushed
¾ cup oyster sauce

1. Cook the noodles in a large pot of boiling water according to packet instructions. Drain and set aside.
2. Place a medium saucepan of water on high heat and bring to the boil. Blanch the gai lan for 1 minute and drain.
3. Preheat a large non-stick frying pan (skillet) or wok on high heat.
4. Add the chicken and cook for 2 minutes or until browned. Add the noodles, gai lan (Chinese broccoli), garlic and oyster sauce and toss to combine. Cook for a further 5 minutes or until chicken is cooked and sauce is heated through.

Serves 4 • Preparation 15 minutes • Cooking 10 minutes

Dukkah lamb racks with smoky mash

4 large eggplants (aubergines)
3 cloves garlic, crushed
300g/10½ oz potatoes, peeled and coarsely chopped
4 racks of lamb, French-trimmed, about 250g/9 oz each
¼ cup dukkah

1. Preheat the grill (broiler) to high.
2. Preheat the oven to 190°C/380°F.
3. Prick the eggplants (aubergines) with a fork, then place on a baking tray (sheet) with the garlic. Grill, turning occasionally, for 15 minutes until skin has blackened and insides are tender. Remove eggplants and garlic and set aside to cool. Cut the eggplants in half lengthwise. Scoop the flesh out into a medium bowl, add the garlic and mash with a fork. Set aside and keep warm.
4. Meanwhile, place the potatoes in a medium saucepan. Cover with cold water and bring to the boil. Cook for 5–10 minutes or until tender. Drain, return to the saucepan and mash. Add the eggplant and stir to combine.
5. Coat the lamb in dukkah and roast for 25 minutes for medium or until cooked to your liking. Transfer to a plate, cover and rest for 5 minutes. Serve with smoky mash.

Dukkah is an Egyptian dry spice mixture of chopped nuts and seeds.

Serves 4 • Preparation 15 minutes • Cooking 50 minutes

BALSAMIC LAMB WITH BABY BEET SALAD

700g/25 oz lamb fillets
1 teaspoon garlic salt
⅓ cup balsamic vinegar, plus 2 tablespoons
12 baby beetroots, with leaves
150g/5 oz marinated fetta

1 Place the lamb, garlic salt and ⅓ cup of the balsamic vinegar in a medium bowl Cover and refrigerate for 2 hours or until required.
2 Place a medium saucepan of salted water on high heat and bring to the boil.
3 Cut the baby beetroots from their stems. Boil the beets for 20–30 minutes or until tender. Drain and set aside to cool.
4 Wash and trim the beetroot leaves and place in a medium bowl.
5 Peel the beets, cut in half and add to the leaves. Crumble the fetta and add to the salad. Combine 1 tablespoon of the oil from the fetta with the 2 tablespoons balsamic vinegar in a small bowl. Add to the salad and toss to combine.
6 Preheat a barbecue chargrill (charbroiler) to medium.
7 Cook the lamb for 4 minutes on each side for medium, or until cooked to your liking. Transfer to a plate, cover and rest for 5 minutes.
8 Divide the salad amongst four serving plates. Slice the lamb and arrange on top.

Serves 4 • Preparation 2 hours 10 minutes • Cooking 40 minutes

Five-spice barbecued pork

⅓ cup hoisin sauce
4 tablespoons Chinese five-spice powder
3 pork fillets, about 350g/12 oz each
2 bunches baby bok choy, cut in half lengthwise
¼ cup water

1. Combine the hoisin sauce and five-spice powder in a medium bowl. Add the pork, stir to coat, cover and refrigerate for 2 hours or until required.
2. Preheat a barbecue chargrill (charbroiler) to medium.
3. Cook the pork for 5–6 minutes on each side or until cooked to your liking. Transfer to a plate, cover and rest for 5 minutes.
4. Meanwhile, heat water in a wok over high heat. Cook the bok choy for 1–2 minutes or until tender.
5. Thickly slice the pork fillet and serve with the bok choy.

Serves 4 • Preparation 2 hours 5 minutes • Cooking 15 minutes

Pork stir-fry

600g/21 oz pork fillet, thinly sliced
2 x 425g/15 oz canned baby corn spears, drained
1 teaspoon plum sauce
½ cup char siu sauce
200g/7 oz snowpeas (mange tout), trimmed

1. Preheat a large non-stick frying pan (skillet) or wok on high heat.
2. Cook the pork, stirring occasionally, for 3 minutes or until browned. Add the baby corn, plum and char siu sauces and cook for 2 minutes. Add the snowpeas (mange tout), cook for a further 1–2 minutes and toss to combine.
3. Divide the pork stir-fry evenly amongst four serving bowls.

Char siu sauce is a specialty barbecue sauce made with soy sauce, honey, sugar, dry sherry, salt, Chinese five-spice powder and crushed fresh ginger (gingeroot).

Serves 4 • Preparation 10 minutes • Cooking 10 minutes

Ginger pork noodles

400g/14 oz udon noodles
1 tablespoon vegetable oil
600g/21 oz pork fillet, thinly sliced
5cm/2 in piece fresh ginger (gingerroot), peeled and grated
⅓ cup oyster sauce

1. Place a medium saucepan of water on high heat and bring to the boil. Cook the noodles according to the packet directions and drain.
2. Heat the oil in a large non-stick frying pan (skillet) or wok on medium-high heat.
3. Cook the pork and ginger (gingerroot), stirring occasionally, for 5 minutes or until browned. Add the oyster sauce and cook for a further 5 minutes. Add the noodles and toss to combine.
4. Divide the ginger pork noodles evenly amongst four serving bowls.

Serves 4 • Preparation 10 minutes • Cooking 15 minutes

Beef fillet wrapped in prosciutto with mash

1kg/2 lb sweet potato (yam), peeled and coarsely chopped
1 teaspoon ground nutmeg
4 beef fillet steaks, about 180g/6½ oz each
8 slices prosciutto
2 tablespoons wholegrain mustard

1. Preheat the oven to 190°C/380°F.
2. Place the sweet potato (yam) in a medium saucepan, cover with cold water and bring to the boil. Cook for 10 minutes or until tender. Drain, return to the saucepan and mash with the nutmeg. Keep warm.
3. Meanwhile, preheat a large non-stick frying pan (skillet) on high heat.
4. Cook the steaks for 1 minute on each side or until browned. Remove from the heat and allow to cool slightly.
5. Wrap two pieces of prosciutto around each beef fillet, securing with a toothpick.
6. Place the beef on a baking tray (sheet) and bake for 8–10 minutes or until done to your liking. Transfer to a plate, cover and rest for 5 minutes.
7. Serve the beef fillets with sweet potato mash and wholegrain mustard.

Serves 4 • Preparation 15 minutes • Cooking 25 minutes

Beef fillet with wild mushroom ragù

2 teaspoons vegetable oil
4 beef fillet steaks, about 180g/6½ oz each
400g/14 oz mixed wild mushrooms
⅓ cup beef stock (broth)
⅓ cup thickened (whipping) cream

1 Preheat the oven to 190°C/380°F.
2 Heat the oil in a large non-stick frying pan (skillet) on medium-high heat.
3 Cook the steaks for 4–5 minutes on each side or until done to your liking. Transfer to a plate, cover and rest for 5 minutes.
4 In the same pan, cook the mushrooms, stirring, for 3 minutes or until golden brown. Add the beef stock (broth) and cream and bring to the boil. Decrease the heat and simmer for 2 minutes or until thickened slightly.
5 Serve the beef topped with the mushroom ragù.

Serves 4 • Preparation 5 minutes • Cooking 20 minutes

Mustard Roast Beef

1½kg/3⅓ lb beef fillet, trimmed of fat
¼ cup olive oil
1 clove garlic, crushed
½ cup wholegrain mustard
1kg/2 lb baby (new) potatoes

1. Preheat the oven to 200°C/400°F.
2. Preheat a large non-stick frying pan (skillet) on high heat.
3. Brush the beef fillet with 3 tablespoons olive oil and crushed garlic and cook, turning occasionally, for 5 minutes or until browned all over.
4. Transfer to a large roasting dish. Rub the mustard over the beef and bake for 40 minutes for medium-rare, or until cooked to your liking. Remove from the oven, cover and rest for 10 minutes.
5. Meanwhile, place the potatoes in a large saucepan, cover with cold water and bring to the boil. Cook for 10 minutes or until tender. Drain.
6. Heat the remaining oil in a large frying pan. Add the potatoes and cook for 3–4 minutes or until golden brown.
7. Slice the beef fillet and serve with the potatoes.

Serves 8 • Preparation 10 minutes • Cooking 1 hour 10 minutes

Sichuan beef stir-fry

1 tablespoon vegetable oil
600g/21 oz beef tenderloin, thinly sliced
1½ teaspoons Sichuan pepper
2 bunches gai lan (Chinese broccoli), cut into 5cm/2 in lengths
½ cup char siu sauce

1 Heat the oil in a large non-stick frying pan (skillet) or wok on high heat.
2 Place the beef and Sichuan pepper in a medium bowl and stir to combine. Add the beef to the pan and cook, stirring occasionally, for 1–2 minutes or until browned. Add the gai lan and cook for a further 2 minutes. Pour in the char siu sauce, heat through and toss to combine.
3 Divide the beef stir-fry evenly amongst four serving bowls.

Char siu sauce is a specialty barbecue sauce made with soy sauce, honey, sugar, dry sherry, salt, Chinese five-spice powder and crushed fresh ginger (gingeroot).

Serves 4 • Preparation 10 minutes • Cooking 5 minutes

PASTA & RICE

PASTA & RICE

PASTA & RICE

Rice, the mainstay of half the world's population, is so easy to cook – just steam or boil and it's ready. Rice goes with everything, so it's incredibly simple to vary the flavour with nothing more than the addition of this or that ingredient. Pasta is almost equally versatile, and all the recipes in this chapter have been developed with the express purpose of making a tasty meal with a minimum of fuss, time and ingredients. Many pastas are also interchangeable – if the recipe calls for spaghetti but you use the fettuccine you already had in the cupboard, the recipe will still taste just as great.

LINGUINE WITH PESTO CREAM

500g/18 oz linguine
1¼ cups thickened (whipping) cream
4 sprigs parsley, finely chopped
½ cup basil pesto
80g/2¾ oz Parmesan cheese, shaved

1. Bring a large saucepan of salted water to the boil, add the pasta and cook for 8 minutes or until just firm in the centre (al dente).
2. Meanwhile, place the cream, parsley and pesto in a large non-stick frying pan (skillet) over medium heat. Gently simmer, stirring occasionally, for 3–4 minutes until thickened slightly.
3. Drain the pasta and return to the pan in which it was cooked. Pour over the pesto cream and toss to combine.
4. Divide the pasta amongst four serving bowls and top with Parmesan to serve.

Serves 4 • Preparation 5 minutes • Cooking 15 minutes

Spinach and ricotta ravioli with tomato sauce

800g/28 oz canned diced Roma tomatoes
¼ cup parsley, finely chopped
½ cup fresh basil leaves, finely chopped
500g/18 oz spinach and ricotta ravioli
80g/2¾ oz pecorino cheese, shaved

1. Place the tomatoes, parsley and basil in a medium heavy-based saucepan over medium-low heat. Gently simmer for 20 minutes or until sauce has thickened and flavours infused.
2. Bring a large saucepan of salted water to the boil, add the pasta and cook for 8 minutes or until just firm in the centre (al dente). Drain the pasta and divide evenly amongst four serving bowls. Top with tomato sauce and pecorino cheese.

Serves 4 • Preparation 5 minutes • Cooking 30 minutes

Smoked Salmon and Lemon Pappardelle

500g/18 oz pappardelle
½ cup olive oil
1 clove garlic, crushed
juice and finely grated zest of 2 lemons
250g/9 oz smoked salmon, coarsely chopped

1. Bring a large saucepan of salted water to the boil, add the pasta and cook for 8 minutes or until just firm in the centre (al dente).
2. Meanwhile, heat the olive oil, garlic, lemon juice and zest in a large frying pan (skillet) over medium-low heat.
3. Drain the pasta and add to the pan. Add the smoked salmon and toss to combine.
4. Divide evenly amongst four serving bowls and serve immediately.

Serves 4 • Preparation 5 minutes • Cooking 15 minutes

Capellini with Fresh Tomato Sauce

500g/18 oz capellini
12 tomatoes, chopped
1 teaspoon lemon juice
½ cup extra virgin olive oil
¾ cup fresh basil leaves, torn

1. Bring a large saucepan of salted water to the boil, add the pasta and cook for 8 minutes or until just firm in the centre (al dente).
2. Meanwhile, place the tomatoes, lemon juice, oil and basil in a medium bowl. Stir to combine.
3. Drain the pasta and return to the pan in which it was cooked. Stir through the sauce.
4. Divide evenly amongst four serving bowls.

Serves 4 • Preparation 5 minutes • Cooking 15 minutes

Spaghetti with Anchovies and Lemon

500g/18 oz spaghetti
50g/1¾ oz anchovies in oil, coarsely chopped
juice and finely grated zest of 2 lemons
1 clove garlic, crushed
1 cup flat-leaf parsley, chopped

1. Bring a large saucepan of salted water to the boil, add the pasta and cook for 8 minutes or until just firm in the centre (al dente). Drain, set aside and keep warm.
2. Place a large non-stick frying pan (skillet) on medium-high heat. Add the anchovies and oil, lemon juice and zest, garlic and parsley, and warm through. Add the pasta and toss to combine.
3. Divide the pasta evenly amongst four serving bowls.

Serves 4 • Preparation 10 minutes • Cooking 15 minutes

Tortellini with Sage Butter

500g/18 oz meat-filled tortellini
100g/3½ oz butter
¾ cup fresh sage leaves
½ teaspoon freshly ground black pepper
80g/2¾ oz Parmesan cheese, grated

1. Bring a large saucepan of salted water to the boil, add the pasta and cook for 8 minutes or until just firm in the centre (al dente).
2. Meanwhile, melt the butter in a large frying pan (skillet) over medium-high heat. Add the sage and black pepper and cook for 30 seconds or until fragrant.
3. Drain the pasta and add to the sage butter. Toss to combine. Divide evenly amongst four serving bowls, top with Parmesan and serve.

Serves 4 • Preparation 5 minutes • Cooking 15 minutes

Squid Ink Pasta with Garlic Seafood

500g/18 oz squid ink pasta
½ cup extra virgin olive oil
6 cloves garlic, minced
24 prawns (shrimp), peeled and deveined
freshly ground black pepper

1 Bring a large saucepan of salted water to the boil, add the pasta and cook for 8 minutes or until just firm in the centre (al dente). Drain, set aside and keep warm.
2 Place a large frying pan (skillet) on medium-low heat. Add the oil and garlic and gently sauté for 2 minutes or until garlic softens.
3 Increase the heat to medium-high and cook the prawns (shrimp) for 1½ minutes on each side or until they turn pink and begin to firm up. Add the pasta to the pan and toss to combine. Sprinkle black pepper over and mix through.
4 Divide the pasta evenly amongst four serving bowls.

Serves 4 • Preparation 10 minutes • Cooking 15 minutes

Pumpkin risotto

1¼ kg/2¾ lb pumpkin, peeled and cut into 3cm/1¼ in cubes
400g/14 oz Arborio rice
4½ cups chicken stock (broth), heated
1 teaspoon crème fraîche
120g/4¼ oz Parmesan cheese, freshly grated

1 Preheat the oven to 200°C/400°F.
2 Place the pumpkin on an oven tray (sheet) and bake for 20–30 minutes or until soft and golden.
3 Meanwhile, preheat a medium saucepan over medium-low heat. Add the rice and cook, stirring, for 1 minute. Reduce the heat to low, add ½ cup hot stock (broth) and cook, stirring constantly, until liquid is absorbed. Continue cooking in this way until all the stock is used and the rice is creamy and tender.
4 Add the pumpkin, crème fraîche and half the Parmesan to the risotto and stir through to warm and combine.
5 Divide the risotto evenly amongst four serving bowls and top with the remaining Parmesan to serve.

Serves 4 • Preparation 10 minutes • Cooking 40–50 minutes

Mushroom and Pea Pilaf

200g/7 oz Swiss brown mushrooms, sliced
2 cups basmati rice
3 cups chicken stock (broth)
finely ground black pepper
1 cup frozen peas

1 Preheat a medium saucepan over medium heat. Add the mushroom and cook for 1–2 minutes. Add the rice and stock (broth) and bring to the boil. Reduce the heat to low, cover and cook for 20 minutes or until all the liquid has been absorbed.

2 Remove from the heat, add pepper and the peas and set aside, covered, for an additional 5 minutes. Stir through to combine and separate the grains. Divide evenly amongst four serving bowls.

Serves 4 • Preparation 5 minutes • Cooking 30 minutes

Pineapple coconut rice

2 cups basmati rice
300g/10½ oz fresh pineapple, peeled and diced
½ cup fresh coriander (cilantro) leaves
½ cup fresh mint leaves, finely sliced
¼ cup coconut milk

1. Combine the rice with 3 cups water in a saucepan. Bring to the boil, reduce heat to low, cover and cook for 15 minutes. Remove pan from heat, allow to stand covered for 10 minutes.
2. Spread the rice out on a tray. Refrigerate for 20 minutes or until cooled.
3. Place the rice, pineapple, coriander (cilantro), mint and coconut milk in a large bowl, stir to combine and serve.

Serves 4 • Preparation 30 minutes • Cooking 15 minutes

Pistachio and Saffron Rice

2½ cups salted water
2 cups basmati rice
pinch of saffron threads
1 cup pistachios, coarsely chopped
¼ cup currants

1. Place salted water in a medium saucepan and bring to the boil. Add the rice and saffron and bring back to the boil. Reduce the heat to low, cover and simmer for 10 minutes. Remove from the heat and set aside with the lid on for a further 10 minutes.
2. Add the pistachios and currants and stir through to combine and separate the grains.
3. Divide evenly amongst four serving bowls.

Serves 4 • Preparation 5 minutes • Cooking 25 minutes

VEGETARIAN

VEGETARIAN

With a terrific range of vegetables available all year round it is easy to select a series of recipes to please any palate – the hard part is to make them interesting using only a small number of additional ingredients. But don't worry, as we have developed the recipes in this chapter using a minimum of ingredients for maximum taste. They can be used as an addition to a meal or as a meal in their own right.

Asparagus and Tofu Miso Soup

1½ litres/6¼ cups vegetable stock (broth)
1 teaspoon salt
¼ cup white miso paste
1 bunch asparagus, trimmed and cut into 4cm/1½ in lengths
400g/14 oz silken tofu, cut into 2cm/¾ in cubes

1. Place the stock (broth) and salt in a medium saucepan over medium-high heat and bring to the boil. Decrease the heat to low. Ladle ¼ cup of stock into a heatproof jug. Add the miso paste and stir until combined, then pour back into the stock.
2. Add the asparagus and tofu to the stock and cook for 2–3 minutes until asparagus is just tender.
3. Ladle the soup into four serving bowls.

Serves 4 • Preparation 5 minutes • Cooking 10 minutes

Baked Eggplant and Ricotta Rolls

2 medium eggplants (aubergines)
750g/1½ lb ricotta cheese
¾ cup fresh basil, finely chopped
700g/25 oz passata (tomato purée)
½ teaspoon mixed herbs

1. Preheat the oven to 200°C/400°F.
2. Cut the eggplants (aubergines) lengthwise into 1cm/⅓ in-thick slices. Arrange the eggplant in a single layer on 2 large baking trays (sheets). Bake for 10 minutes or until golden.
3. Meanwhile, place 600g/21 oz of the ricotta and ½ cup of the basil in a medium bowl and stir to combine.
4. Place a spoonful of ricotta mixture on an eggplant slice and roll up to enclose the filling. Place the roll seam-side down in a 30 x 20cm/12 x 8 in baking dish. Repeat the process with the remaining ricotta mixture and eggplant.
5. Pour the passata (tomato purée) over the eggplant rolls. Sprinkle the remaining ricotta and basil over the top. Bake for 15 minutes or until heated through and ricotta is golden.

Passata is puréed and strained tomatoes without seasonings. It should be readily available from your local supermarket.

Serves 4 • Preparation 15 minutes • Cooking 25 minutes

SPANISH TORTILLA

750g/1½ lb potatoes, thinly sliced
⅓ cup olive oil
1 large brown onion, sliced
1 clove garlic, crushed
6 large eggs, lightly beaten

1. Preheat the grill (broiler) to medium-high.
2. Place the potato slices in a large saucepan and cover with cold water. Bring to the boil and cook for 2 minutes. Drain.
3. Place the oil in a large, non-stick, flameproof frying pan (skillet) over medium-high heat. Add the onion, garlic and potato slices and cook, stirring, for 4–5 minutes or until browned. Decrease the heat to low and pour in the beaten eggs. Cook without stirring for 4–6 minutes or until edges are firm.
4. Place the pan under the grill and cook for a further 4–6 minutes or until the egg is set and golden.
5. Cut the tortilla into portions to serve.

Serves 4 • Preparation 10 minutes • Cooking 20 minutes

TOMATOES STUFFED WITH RICE

½ cup long-grain rice
4 large tomatoes
100g/3½ oz mozzarella cheese, diced
30g/1 oz Parmesan cheese, grated
⅓ cup fresh basil, finely chopped

1. Preheat the oven to 180°C/360°F.
2. Place the rice and 1 cup cold water in a small saucepan over high heat and bring to the boil. Reduce the heat to medium-low, cover and simmer for 12 minutes. Remove from the heat and stir through to separate the grains.
3. Meanwhile, cut the tops off the tomatoes and set aside. Scoop out the flesh and coarsely chop. Place the tomato flesh, mozzarella, Parmesan and basil in a medium bowl. Add the rice and stir to combine.
4. Place the tomato shells on a baking tray (sheet) and fill with the rice mixture. Put their tops back on and bake for 25–30 minutes until tomatoes are tender but still hold their shape.
5. Serve warm or cold.

Serves 4 • Preparation 10 minutes • Cooking 45 minutes

Polenta slices with roasted pesto tomatoes

1 litre/4¼ cups vegetable stock (broth)
1 cup instant polenta (cornmeal)
18 medium vine-ripened tomatoes
¾ cup basil pesto
½ teaspoon lemon pepper

1. Line a 20 x 30cm/8 x 12 in shallow baking tray (sheet) with baking paper.
2. Place the stock (broth) in a medium saucepan over medium-high heat and bring to the boil. Decrease the heat to medium-low. Pour in the polenta (cornmeal), whisking until it begins to thicken. Stirring constantly with a wooden spoon, cook for a further 3 minutes. Pour the polenta into the prepared tray and smooth over the surface. Leave to cool slightly. Refrigerate for 30 minutes or until firm.
3. Preheat the oven to 190°C/380°F.
4. Place the tomatoes on a large baking tray and bake for 15 minutes or until they begin to soften.
5. Meanwhile, preheat a chargrill (charbroil) plate to medium-high.
6. Cut the polenta into 6 even-sized pieces. Brush the polenta with a little of the pesto and lemon pepper mixed together and grill for 2–3 minutes on each side until charred and crisp.
7. To serve, place a piece of grilled polenta onto each plate. Spread over the remaining pesto, then top with roasted tomatoes.

Serves 6 • Preparation 40 minutes • Cooking 30 minutes

VEGETARIAN PAD THAI

200g/7 oz rice noodles
4 large eggs, lightly beaten
⅓ cup pad Thai paste
250g/9 oz firm tofu, cut into 3cm/1¼ in cubes
1 teaspoon olive oil

1. Place the noodles in a medium heatproof bowl. Cover with boiling water and set aside for 10–15 minutes or until softened, then drain.
2. Meanwhile, preheat a large non-stick frying pan (skillet) or wok on medium heat. Add the egg and swirl to coat. Cook for 2 minutes or until set. Transfer to a plate, roll up and chop roughly.
3. Add the pad Thai paste and tofu to the pan and cook for 1 minute or until aromatic. Add the noodles and cook for a further minute to warm through. Add the egg and olive oil and toss to combine.
4. Divide the noodles evenly amongst four serving bowls.

Serves 4 • Preparation 5 minutes • Cooking 20 minutes

VEGETARIAN NACHOS

2 x 400g/14 oz canned Mexican beans
300g/10½ oz mild tomato salsa dip
1 teaspoon minced onion
250g/9 oz corn (nacho) chips
150g/5 oz cheddar cheese, grated

1. Preheat the oven to 190°C/380°F.
2. Place the beans, salsa and onion in a small saucepan over medium heat. Gently simmer for 3–4 minutes or until thickened slightly.
3. Arrange half of the corn (nacho) chips in the base of four individual ovenproof serving bowls. Spoon half of the bean mixture on top and cover with the remaining chips. Top with the remaining bean mixture and sprinkle with cheese.
4. Bake for 5–10 minutes, until the cheese has melted.
5. Serve immediately, being careful with the hot bowls.

Serves 4 • Preparation 5 minutes • Cooking 15 minutes

Broccoli and Gruyère quiche

1 sheet ready-rolled shortcrust pastry, thawed
500g/18 oz broccoli, cut into florets
200g/7 oz Gruyère cheese, thinly sliced
8 large eggs, lightly beaten
1 tablespoon cream

1 Preheat the oven to 200°C/400°F.

2 Line a 23cm/9 in springform tart pan with pastry. Cover the pastry case with a sheet of baking paper and fill with rice or baking beads. Place on a baking tray (sheet) and bake for 5–10 minutes until base is lightly golden. Remove the baking paper and weights and set aside.

3 Place a medium saucepan of water on high heat and bring to the boil Cook the broccoli for 1–2 minutes or until just tender, then drain.

4 Arrange the broccoli in the pastry case. Top with cheese and pour in the egg mixed with the cream.

5 Bake for 30–35 minutes until set. Stand for 10 minutes.

Serves 6 • Preparation 15 minutes • Cooking 55 minutes

Mushroom Stroganoff

500g/18 oz fettuccine
1 large brown onion, sliced
800g/28 oz button mushrooms, sliced
1¼ cups crème fraîche
¼ cup thickened (whipping) cream

1. Bring a large saucepan of salted water to the boil, add the pasta and cook for 8 minutes or until just firm in the centre (al dente). Drain, set aside and keep warm.
2. Meanwhile, place a large non-stick frying pan (skillet) on medium heat. Cook the onion and mushrooms, stirring occasionally, for 5 minutes or until softened and golden. Add the crème fraîche and cream, and stir to combine. Decrease the heat to medium-low and gently simmer for 5 minutes or until sauce has thickened slightly.
3. Divide the pasta evenly amongst four serving bowls and top with sauce.

Serves 4 • Preparation 10 minutes • Cooking 20 minutes

DESSERTS

DESSERTS

Let's not forget one of the most anticipated courses in your repertoire. We have come to the rescue with a brilliant selection of easy-to-prepare dishes, with each one a taste sensation, yet still using only five ingredients. Don't worry about the kilojoules or a long preparation time – these recipes can be on the table in less than 10 minutes and devoured in less time than that, with satisfied smiles all around.

CHOCOLATE PROFITEROLES

250g/9 oz dark (semi-sweet) chocolate
1¼ cups thickened (whipping) cream
1 teaspoon vanilla extract
¼ teaspoon orange blossom water
12 profiterole puffs

1. Melt the chocolate and ¼ cup of the cream together in a small heatproof bowl over a saucepan of barely simmering water. Stir to combine and set aside to cool.
2. Whip the remaining cream with the vanilla and orange blossom water in a small bowl using an electric mixer until soft peaks form. Spoon the cream into a pastry bag fitted with a round nozzle.
3. Cut a hole big enough to fit the piping nozzle in the base of the profiterole cases. Pipe cream into the profiteroles and divide evenly amongst four serving plates.
4. Drizzle chocolate sauce over the top and serve immediately.

Profiteroles can be bought ready-made from a bakery or your local supermarket.

Serves 4 • Preparation 15 minutes

Berry Eton Mess

250g/9 oz fresh raspberries
250g/9 oz fresh strawberries
2 tablespoons icing (confectioner's) sugar
1½ cups thickened (whipping) cream
4 small meringues

1. Place half the berries in a food processor. Add the icing (confectioner's) sugar and blend until puréed. Strain through a fine mesh sieve and discard the seeds.
2. Whip the cream in a medium bowl until soft peaks form. Add the remaining berries and stir to combine.
3. Crush the meringues and place in a medium bowl. Add the berry cream and half of the berry purée and stir to just combine.
4. To serve, spoon the meringue mixture into four serving bowls or glasses and drizzle with the remaining berry purée.

Serves 4 • Preparation 15 minutes

Chocolate mousse

3 large eggs, separated
3 teaspoons dark brown sugar
100g/3½ oz dark (semi-sweet) chocolate
1 teaspoon olive oil
1½ cups thickened (whipping) cream

1. Whisk the egg yolks and sugar together in a small heatproof bowl. Place the bowl over a saucepan of barely simmering water and continue whisking until thick and creamy. Remove from the heat.
2. Put the chocolate in a small heatproof bowl and place over the simmering water to melt, whisk olive oil into the melted chocolate and pour into the egg yolk mixture, stir to combine and set aside to cool.
3. Whip 1 cup of the cream in a small bowl until soft peaks form. In a separate bowl, whisk the egg whites until soft peaks form. Fold the cream and whites together.
4. Stir 1 tablespoonful of the egg white mixture into the chocolate. Add the remaining egg white mixture and gently fold until combined. Pour the mousse into serving cups or bowls. Cover with plastic wrap and refrigerate for 2 hours or until required.
5. Whip the remaining cream in a small bowl. Spoon into a pastry bag fitted with a star nozzle. Pipe a small amount on top of each mousse. Decorate with shaved extra chocolate.

Serves 4 • Preparation 2 hours 25 minutes

CHERRY STRUDEL

2 x 425g/15 oz canned pitted black cherries in syrup, drained
½ teaspoon kirsch liqueur
100g/3½ oz ground almonds
4 sheets filo pastry
50g/1¾ oz butter, melted

1. Preheat the oven to 200°C/400°F.
2. Place the cherries, kirsch and ground almonds in a medium bowl and stir to combine.
3. Lay one sheet of filo on a clean surface. Brush with melted butter. Top with another layer of filo and repeat until all the sheets of pastry are layered.
4. Brush a large baking tray (sheet) with melted butter and place the filo sheets on top.
5. Spread the cherry mixture down one side of the filo. Fold the pastry over, sealing the edges and brushing the top with melted butter.
6. Place strudel in the oven and bake for 20–25 minutes or until golden brown.
7. Cut into portions and serve warm.

Serves 4 • Preparation 15 minutes • Cooking 25 minutes

Jaffa sorbet

1 cup caster (berry) sugar
1 cup cocoa powder
zest of 2 oranges
juice of 1 orange
½ teaspoon orange liqueur

1. Place 2¾ cups water and the sugar in a medium saucepan over medium-high heat and bring to the boil. Reduce the heat and simmer, stirring occasionally, until the sugar has dissolved.
2. Add the cocoa powder, orange zest, orange juice and orange liqueur and simmer gently for 15 minutes. Remove from the heat and strain through a fine mesh sieve. Discard the orange zest.
3. Refrigerate until cooled.
4. Pour the cooled liquid into an ice maker and churn until the sorbet (sherbet) starts to become firm. Serve immediately or transfer to a container and freeze until required.

Serves 4 • Preparation 1 hour

ZABAGLIONE

4 large egg yolks
¼ cup caster (berry) sugar
¼ teaspoon vanilla extract
¼ cup Marsala or dessert wine
8 sponge fingers

1 Place the egg yolks, sugar and vanilla in a medium heatproof bowl. Whisk the yolks until thick and creamy. Gradually add the Marsala, whisking to combine.
2 Place the bowl over a saucepan of barely simmering water. Cook, whisking continuously, for 10 minutes, until thick enough to coat the back of a spoon.
3 Pour into 4 serving glasses. Serve immediately with sponge fingers on the side.

Serves 4 • Preparation 5 minutes • Cooking 10 minutes

Chocolate and Hazelnut Tart

1 sheet ready-rolled shortcrust pastry, thawed
250g/9 oz dark (semi-sweet) chocolate
1 cup thickened (whipping) cream
1 cup hazelnuts, lightly toasted and coarsely chopped
½ teaspoon hazelnut liqueur

1. Preheat the oven to 180°C/360°F.
2. Line a 20cm/8 in springform tart pan with the pastry. Refrigerate for 10 minutes.
3. Cover the pastry case with a sheet of baking paper and fill with rice or baking beads. Place on a baking tray (sheet) and bake for 5–10 minutes until base is lightly golden. Remove the baking paper and weights and bake for a further 10 minutes or until the centre is cooked through. Set aside to cool.
4. Meanwhile, put the chocolate and cream into a small heatproof bowl. Place over a saucepan of barely simmering water and melt, stirring occasionally until smooth. Stir ¾ cup of the hazelnuts and the liqueur into the chocolate mixture and pour into the prepared pastry case. Refrigerate for 2 hours or until set.
5. Decorate the tart with the remaining hazelnuts.

Serves 6–8 • Preparation 2 hours 15 minutes • Cooking 20 minutes

Vanilla Crème Brûlée

2½ cups thickened (whipping) cream
1 vanilla pod, split lengthwise
6 large egg yolks
½ cup caster (berry) sugar
1 teaspoon finely grated orange zest

1. Preheat the oven to 120°C/250°F.
2. Place the cream, vanilla pod and seeds in a small saucepan over medium heat and bring to scalding point. Remove from the heat and set aside to infuse for 10 minutes.
3. Meanwhile, place the egg yolks and half the sugar in a medium bowl. Whisk until pale and creamy.
4. Remove the vanilla pod from the cream and discard. Gradually pour the hot cream into the egg mixture, stirring with a wooden spoon to combine. Strain the custard mixture through a fine mesh sieve and mix through orange zest.
5. Pour the custard into four 150mL/5 fl oz ovenproof ramekins. Place the ramekins in a deep roasting pan. Pour boiling water into the pan to come halfway up the side of the ramekins, then cover the pan loosely with foil. Place in the oven and bake for 40 minutes or until custards are set but still slightly wobbly.
6. Carefully remove the ramekins from the pan and set aside to cool. Cover with plastic wrap and refrigerate for 4 hours or until required.
7. Preheat the grill (broiler) to high.
8. Sprinkle the remaining sugar evenly over the top of the custards. Place under the grill and caramelise. Alternatively, you can use a domestic blow torch to caramelise. Serve immediately.

Serves 4 • Preparation 4 hours 30 minutes • Cooking 40 minutes

Lemon Mille-Feuille

2 sheets ready-rolled puff pastry, thawed
½ cup thickened (whipping) cream
½ teaspoon lemon juice
½ cup lemon curd
1 tablespoon icing (confectioner's) sugar

1 Preheat the oven to 200°C/400°F.
2 Cut each pastry sheet into six 6 x 12cm/2½ x 5 in rectangles. Lay the pastry on two baking trays (sheets) and bake for 10–15 minutes until puffed and golden brown. Remove from the oven, flatten slightly and leave to cool.
3 Whip the cream in a small bowl until soft peaks form. Add the lemon juice to the lemon curd and stir to combine. Mix lemon curd mixture into cream.
4 Spread half of the lemon cream over four pieces of the pastry. Top with another piece of pastry and repeat the process, finishing with the last pastry sheet.
5 Dust with icing (confectioner's) sugar and serve immediately.

Serves 4 • Preparation 15 minutes • Cooking 15 minutes

Custard tart

1 sheet ready-rolled shortcrust pastry, thawed
1 cup milk
½ cup cream
2 large eggs, plus 1 large egg yolk
2 tablespoons caster (berry) sugar

1. Preheat the oven to 180°C/360°F.
2. Line a 6cm/2½ in deep by 20cm/8 in round springform tart pan with the pastry. Refrigerate for 10 minutes.
3. Cover the pastry case with a sheet of baking paper and fill with rice or pie weights. Place on a baking tray (sheet) and bake for 5–10 minutes until base is lightly golden. Remove baking paper and weights and set aside.
4. Reduce the oven temperature to 160°C/320°F.
5. Place the milk, cream, eggs, egg yolk and sugar in a medium bowl and whisk to combine. Pour the mixture into the tart base and return to the oven to cook for 20 minutes or until custard is set. Remove from the oven and leave to cool for 10 minutes. Refrigerate for 2 hours or until required.

Serves 6 • Preparation 2 hours 10 minutes • Cooking 40 minutes

Weights and Measures

Although recipes have been tested using the Australian Standard 250ml cup, 20ml tablespoon and 5ml teaspoon, they will work just as well with the US and Canadian 8fl oz cup, or the UK 300ml cup. We have used graduated cup measures in preference to tablespoon measures so that proportions are always the same. Where tablespoon measures have been given, they are not crucial measures, so using the smaller tablespoon of the US or UK will not affect the recipe's success.But we all agree on the teaspoon size.

For breads, cakes and pastries, the only area which might cause concern is where eggs are used, as proportions will then vary. If working with a 250ml or 300ml cup, use large eggs (65g/2¼ oz), adding a little more liquid to the recipe for 300ml cup measures if it seems necessary. Use medium-sized eggs (60g/2 oz) with an 8fl oz cup measure. A graduated set of measuring cups and spoons is recommended, the cups in particular for measuring dry ingredients. Remember to level such ingredients to ensure an accurate quantity.

Oven Temperatures

The Celsius temperatures given here are not exact; they have been rounded off and are given as a guide only. Follow the manufacturer's temperature guide, relating it to oven description given in the recipe. Remember gas ovens are hottest at the top, electric ovens at the bottom and convection-fan forced ovens are usually even throughout. We've included Regulo numbers for gas cookers, which may assist. To convert °C to °F multiply °C by 9 and divide by 5 then add 32.

	C°	F°	Gas Regulo
Very slow	120	250	1
Slow	150	300	2
Moderately slow	160	320	3
Moderate	180	360	4
Moderately hot	190–200	380–400	5–6
Hot	210–220	410–430	6–7
Very hot	230	450	8
Super hot	250–290	475–550	9–10

English Measures

English measurements are similar to Australian with two exceptions: the English cup measures 300ml/10½fl oz, whereas the American and Australian cup measure 250ml/8¾fl oz. The English tablespoon (the Australian dessertspoon) measures 14.8ml/½ fl oz against the Australian tablespoon of 20ml/¾fl oz.

American Measures

The American tablespoon is equal to 14.8ml/½fl oz, the teaspoon is 5ml/⅙fl oz. The cup measure is 250ml/8¾fl oz.

Dry Measures

All the measures are level, so when you have filled a cup or spoon, level it off with the edge of a knife. The scale below is the 'cook's equivalent'; it is not an exact conversion of metric to imperial measurement. To calculate the exact metric equivalent yourself, multiply ounces by 28.349523 to obtain grams, or divide grams by 28.349523 to obtain ounces.

Metric grams (g), kilograms (kg)	**Imperial** ounces (oz), pound (lb)
15g	½ oz
20g	¾ oz
30g	1 oz
60g	2 oz
90g	3 oz
100g	3½ oz
125g	4 oz
150g	5 oz
170g	6 oz
200g	7 oz
240g	8½ oz
315g	11 oz
350g	12 oz
375g	13 oz
400g	14 oz
425g	15 oz
450g	16 oz
1000g/1kg	2 lb
1½kg	3⅓ lb

Liquid Measures

Metric millilitres (ml)	**Imperial** fluid ounce (fl oz)	**Cup and Spoon**
5ml	⅙ fl oz	1 teaspoon
20ml	⅔ fl oz	1 tablespoon
30ml	1 fl oz	1 tbsp + 2 tsp
55ml	2 fl oz	
63ml	2¼ fl oz	¼ cup
85ml	3 fl oz	
115ml	4 fl oz	
125ml	4½ fl oz	½ cup
150ml	5¼ fl oz	
188ml	6⅔ fl oz	¾ cup
225ml	8¾ fl oz	
250ml	8 fl oz	1 cup
300ml	10½ fl oz	
370ml	13 fl oz	
400ml	14 fl oz	
438ml	15½ fl oz	1¾ cups
455ml	16 fl oz	
500ml	17½ fl oz	2 cups
570ml	20 fl oz	
1 litre	35⅓ fl oz	4 cups

INDEX